Song of
Our Son

Song of
Our Son

BRUCE FRASER

THREE OCEAN PRESS

Library and Archives Canada Cataloguing in Publication

Title: Song of our son / Bruce Fraser.
Names: Fraser, Bruce, 1937- author.
Identifiers: Canadiana 20250254751 | ISBN 9781988915562 (softcover)
Subjects: LCGFT: Poetry.
Classification: LCC PS8611.R366 S66 2025 | DDC C811/.6—dc23

Editor: Kyle Hawke
Cover and Book Designer: PJ Perdue
Proofreader: Carol Hamshaw

Three Ocean Press
8168 Riel Place
Vancouver, BC, V5S 4B3
778.321.0636
info@threeoceanpress.com
www.threeoceanpress.com

First publication, September 2025

For Gail,
to whom
I owe and give
everything

Acknowledgements

My sincerest appreciation goes out to Lauch and Rebecca Fraser, Isabelle and Hugh Morrison, the Honourable Judge G.W.B. Fraser, and Geraldine Fraser, for being with me in times of need.

Contents

Introduction

Bruce Fraser's poems are not polished gemstones. They are stones that have been carried a long way, worn smooth by time, but still bearing the edges and weight of what shaped them. They are beach glass: sharp once, now softened, and catching the light of memory. Their value lies not in refinement but in endurance. They hold what the poet could not bear to forget. They are fragments gathered and kept, not to impress, but to honour. To mark presence. To say: *I was here. These are the people I have loved. I keep them close in language.*

The collection is wide in scope and intimate in tone. It gathers together love poems and elegies, family portraits and philosophical reflections, meditations on trees, compost heaps, legal cases, and sacred texts. Some poems unfold with warmth and humour, while others reach for something more contemplative. The range of forms is broad, but the sensibility is constant. It is curious, affectionate, sometimes mischievous, and always emotionally sincere. What emerges is a layered accumulation of voices, moods, and memories stitched together by love and persistence.

Across its many voices and settings, the collection creates a mosaic of memory. It captures the ache of grief, the strange joys of domestic life, the unpredictable lessons of nature, and the enduring pull of love. It moves between moments of sacred ritual and the small, familiar gestures that quietly sustain us. In its gathering of seemingly disparate subjects, the collection becomes more than the sum of its parts. It offers not only a record of feeling, but a kind of emotional archaeology: layered, textured, and deeply lived.

The poems move across forms with openness and fluidity. At times the voice is plainspoken. Elsewhere, it turns lyrical or playful. Some lines invite pause through their surprising imagery, others through their emotional clarity. The writing does not reach for easy answers. Instead, it lingers in complexity, listens to silence, and returns to the same questions with tenderness. This is not detachment. It is a sustained gesture of devotion. The writing exists because staying silent would mean letting go.

Fraser's poems are, at heart, acts of conversation. They speak to the dead, to the living, to the reader, and to the past. They return to what cannot be resolved, not to fix it, but to acknowledge it again. They rework memory, grief, humour, and hope into something lasting. That persistence—the quiet and deliberate willingness to ask again—is not a flaw. It is an act of love.

On Grief and Witnessing

The heart of this book is grief. It circles and returns to a lost son again and again. In some poems, he is James; in others, he is Jamie or simply "our son." These shifting names mirror the shifting ground of memory itself, as if the poet is reaching for different registers of intimacy, different tenses of fatherhood. The most affecting moments are often the simplest, the least adorned. In the poem "The Song of Our Son," the narrator recalls: "He waved, flashed a smile, / he opened the truck door, / and he said, 'Hi, Dad, I'm fine. / Good to see you once more.'" The understated language makes no grand claim. It just lets the moment breathe. A son opens a door, says he is fine, and in that gesture lies a whole world of pain, hope, and the unbearable dailiness of mental illness.

Throughout the poem, scenes unfold with painful clarity: coffee at Starbucks, golf games, group home drop-offs. These details are unremarkable, but their quiet repetition gives them weight. They become ritual, a form of attention that turns the ordinary into something enduring. Fraser refuses to romanticize the experience. He returns to it because it was formative, even if unspoken at the time. The regret is quiet, but unmistakable: "I told him he was not alone. / I failed to say that on Wednesdays / he taught me to walk not to run, / be patient with others, / be at peace with myself, / and to speak ill of no one." The son's lesson is not grand or doctrinal. It is behavioural, almost liturgical. A way of moving through the world with care. That he teaches the father, and not the other way around, is not framed as irony. It is simply what happened. In this reversal, there is no sentimental moral. Just the fact of a relationship redefined by need, and by attention. What remains is intimacy, the kind shaped by repetition, observation, and the ache of what was nearly left unsaid.

The poem does not move in a straight line. It circles, pauses, and then abruptly opens into the account of James's final days. The shift is unsettling, almost disorienting, but that disorientation feels intentional. It mirrors the rhythm of real grief, which rarely arrives with clarity or order. What we are given is a jagged trajectory of fragments struggling toward coherence. In one of the poem's most arresting images, the speaker recalls: "At St. Paul's Hospital / James would not be confined, / he left this life by escaping / through a window in his mind." This line folds narrative into metaphor with striking precision. The "window in his mind" suggests a moment of rupture, but also release. It evokes psychosis, but also possibility. The escape is not literal, yet it carries the full weight of a departure. The metaphor refuses resolution, offering instead a space where contradiction can rest. In that space, sorrow does not harden into despair. It remains open, unfinished.

The poem closes with a return to its central refrain, a quiet invocation that points toward prayer, memory, and the possibility of connection: "Hear the words of prayer, / Sing a song to His Son, / Reach for the unknown, / Peace be with everyone." These lines do not resolve with what has come before. They do not seek to. Instead, they offer rhythm, repetition, and something like blessing. The language moves toward ritual, not as consolation, but as continuity. It suggests that while the grief cannot be answered, it can be voiced. And in voicing, perhaps shared. "The Song of Our Son" is the emotional core of this collection not because of its insistence on presence. It sits with loss without flinching and allows the reader to do the same. It offers company, a presence that, in the face of irreparable grief, may be the most enduring form of care.

Other poems take up the thread, shaping grief into a quiet theology. In "Lament for a Son" Fraser asks, "Could a timeless poem / bring our darling home?" The line holds its answer yet poses the question anyway. The gesture reads as devotion. It is an act of calling out when no reply can come. The poem moves through echoes of Donne, Dante, Browning as scaffolding. These references are not worn as cultural capital; they are what the poet reaches for when nothing else will hold. Through them, Fraser constructs a provisional architecture of mourning, offering the loss a place to live. Toward the close, the poem gives way to land. A white cloud climbs the mountains on a Squamish wind, reaching toward the grieving stone Lions. "Poet's words cannot replace / nature's healing grace." As language recedes, the world responds in its own register.

In "James," grief turns outward. The poem unfolds as a dialogue between two friends seated by English Bay, watching white sails drift across the water as the sun begins to set. One confesses: "I buried my son this morning." The conversation moves through sorrow, guilt, theological doubt, and the poetic lineage of Donne, Dante, and the fragile hope of *Paradiso*. The speaker remains unconvinced. Faith wavers. The poem ends with a line that serves as both encouragement and a plea: "Continue to seek answers and Try, / Try to keep your faith alive." The repetition is effort made audible. It is a line that acknowledges how difficult it is to go on, and how necessary it is to try.

Across these poems, Fraser offers more than tribute. He is keeping a conversation alive, with his son, with memory, with the unanswered questions that follow in the wake of loss. The voice does not try to make sense of what happened. It stays with the details, the moments that linger: a coffee, a gesture, a line half-remembered. This is what elegy offers at its most honest. Even when a poem reaches beyond what it can fully express, it returns to a single, unwavering sentiment: to say, with whatever words remain, you mattered.

Grief, in these pages, is not closure. It is a way of remaining in relationship. A way of continuing to speak, even when no answer comes.

On Love and Clumsiness

There is, throughout the collection, a recurring presence: a beloved partner, sometimes named, sometimes implied. Sometimes she appears as "Her," sometimes as a kind of spirit glimpsed in gardens, on mountains, through mist. In "Mountain Lake," she appears as a sacred figure seen through veils of cloud and grief. The speaker stands at the edge of the lake and sees "Her downcast eyes / reflected in the lake's still waters / under mist-filled skies." Nature becomes both mirror and mourner. The surrounding landscape is transformed into a kind of devotional image, "a portrait / of Madonna's grieving face." The poem moves beyond comparison, drawing on sacred imagery to make space for something irreducible: grief that transcends language and settles in the body. The mountain veil lifts gradually, allowing the speaker to linger in uncertainty: "I waited an hour / for the rising of the cloud. / Did the cosmos / have the power / to unwind her heavenly shroud?" What follows is a subdued shift. As sunlight touches the landscape and birdsong breaks the silence, the speaker moves toward recognition. The natural world does not offer an explanation; instead, it reflects what he already carries: "I find myself a witness / to a homecoming so surreal / that all my six senses feel / what reason tries to conceal." The final couplet is pivotal. The poem's logic emerges through an embodied witnessing, an emotional recognition that moves through image, sound, and sensation. The beloved becomes part of the world's unfolding. This is Fraser's love at its most elevated and most stripped back: a quiet act of attention, sustained long enough for grief to take shape as something almost, but not quite, sacred.

But this tenderness is shaped as much by uncertainty as by reverence. In "Our Mutual Friend," Fraser revisits the beginning of a love story he never quite managed to decipher. The poem opens at a party: he is "dressed like a brave," she wears "a feather in her hair." There is dancing, a spark, and then she vanishes. He finds her outside, with the man who connects them both, but nothing is resolved. Instead, we get a sudden pivot: "In a fit of despair / he took her in his arms, / carried her home, / and proposed to her there." The response is impulsive, slightly comic, and unexplained. Years later, after her death, he turns to that same mutual friend and asks what happened that night. The reply arrives like an unassuming gift: she had said, "I am going to marry my Brave." It is a moment of reassurance, offered too late to answer the questions that endure. The poem dwells in affection, in the strangeness of remembered beginnings. What gives the poem its weight is how it holds contradiction. It is part tribute, part comedy: tender, awkward, unresolved. The mutual friend, once a possible rival, becomes a guest at their wedding and a witness to the story neither of them could fully tell. Love here is not fate, but something shaped slowly, imperfectly, and with feeling. Certainty gives way; devotion remains.

That halting tenderness, shaped by both bewilderment and devotion, shifts in tone but remains steady in spirit in "An Unrepentant Husband," where love appears in daily missteps and hard-won forgiveness. Fraser confesses to self-absorption with a rueful wit: "I drank too much wine at dinner / and woke with an aching head. / Deciding to forego my spousal / duties, I lay in bed instead." The tone is casual, even comic. Yet the final lines turn toward something more revealing: "I deduce that my selfish acts, / dear, bring forth the Saint in you." It is at once an apology and a defence, a deflection and a tribute. And if the speaker stops short of examining what that sainthood might have cost, the poem still betrays something more vulnerable: a sense of inadequacy beside a partner who was, in his eyes, more disciplined, more patient, more luminous. Someone who offered more grace than he always knew how to receive.

These are love letters, too. Not only to a partner or son, but to the past, to landscapes, to friends, to language itself, and to the rituals that shape domestic life. In "Backyard Tree," a fir becomes both witness and participant in the life of a family. The tree is remembered as part of the landscape and as "our friend," "our bard," a keeper of stories and song. Children once circled it chanting "ring around the rosie," their voices turning the tree into a living monument. When it is felled, the loss is marked both with grief and with continuity: "seedlings sprang up / all around." And in the final stanza, it is the children's children who now sing beneath its successors. The original chant has changed— "A-tishoo! A-tishoo! / We all jump up!"—but the scene is recognizable. The poem captures how memory is embedded not only in what we recall, but in what returns, altered but still echoing. In "Hearts and Minds," Fraser writes of a daughter in crisis and of a father trying, and failing at times, to help. The poem opens in admiration, then shifts into deeper waters: "Demons danced in her head for years / as she tried to control her fears." Attempts at logic falter. "To help, I tried reason, then blunder," he admits, before concluding "victory isn't won by blunder / or reason alone, it's won by / what's bred in the bone" That line is the poem's pivot. The speaker steps back, and it is the bond between mother and daughter that carries the rest. The final stanzas turn toward resolution, toward shared strength: "Together they silenced her demons, I could tell." The voice remains humble, but full of wonder. The poems bear witness to survival and honours the love that made it possible. In "Clan Fraser's Grand Tour of Scotland," Fraser traces lineage and legacy through the figure of his grandson. What begins as a playful travelogue, "From the English side of Hadrian's Wall / Jack Fraser heard the bagpipes call," becomes a meditation on ancestry and belonging. Jack, only six months old, is swaddled in tartan and cradled in Scottish landscapes that seem to welcome him home. "The heathered hills of Glen Affrick wild, / welcomed Jack, the six-month-old child." There's whimsy in the voice, but the sentiment is real: to place a child within history is also to bless the future. The final toast, "To Scotland, to Jack, to our clan," brings family together in laughter and recognition, naming each member as part of a lineage that is both cultural and deeply personal.

The writing here favours directness over subtlety. Its aim is to witness. What unifies these poems is less a consistent style than a shared emotional intent: to honour what is and was loved, to mark what was difficult, and to keep speaking through the ordinary acts that give life its shape.

On Humour and Nostalgia

Humour, in this collection, is a mode of expression as central as elegy or reflection. It arrives in rhyme, in anecdote, in theatrical turns of phrase. These poems draw from a recognizably Scottish tradition: playful, performative, fond of a pun, and never afraid of a little sentiment. This is humour meant to be shared aloud, whether around a dinner table, at a family gathering, or beside a field still smouldering from a brush fire. Like a good story told with a twinkle in the eye, it carries both wit and feeling.

No poem captures this better than "Grassfire Dance." It begins with a quiet scene: a man tending a spring fire on a Cariboo hillside. The rhythm is steady, even pastoral: "Smoke curls from the grass, / from the flame's slow dance." But what starts as control quickly becomes chaos. The wind shifts, the fire leaps, and the speaker finds himself gasping, sweating, and scrambling to contain the flames: "I'm fighting the fire, inhaling the smoke / and smothering the flames with a shovel." This could tilt toward drama, but the poem refuses to play it straight.

Instead, it leans into farce. The partner's voice calls him from the cabin above: "Dear, do you dance the grass fire dance, / the latest Cariboo craze?" The line punctures the panic through its offbeat humour. Crisis shifts into choreography, misadventure into memory. When the volunteer firefighters arrive, sirens wailing, the closing image resists both tragedy and triumph, offering something stranger—and more enduring: "Later that night, I recalled the fight / while watching the last embers die / and clearest of all that I recall / is the grass fire dancing high." The fire becomes a character, the event a performance, the memory a keepsake shaped by its surreal intensity. The absurdity does not diminish the moment; it anchors it.

In "Ode to Beef Tenderloin," the tone shifts to mock liturgy. A shared dinner becomes a sacred rite, its arrival described with full epic flourish. The pilgrims arrive "BEARING, IN THEIR OUTSTRETCHED ARMS, / VESSELS FULL OF VIANDS AND POMMES DE TERRE," and dinner is given the gravitas of a religious ceremony. The guests offer thanks in full voice, "SUNG IN SWEET UNISON," before the occasion is sealed with a final Latin benediction. The language may be borrowed from scripture, but the sentiment is rooted in lived connection. The poem does not mock the dinner, it elevates it. And in doing so, it reveals one of Fraser's recurring instincts: to praise the everyday by giving it ceremony. The tone is theatrical, and its underlying emotion is gratitude, rendered through a sense of occasion.

Alongside the comedy, there runs a deep current of nostalgia. These poems often return to earlier decades: baseball games, backyard antics, old cars, young love. They brim with remembered details that celebrate the past for its texture rather than its perfection. In "Ode to a Cement Block Compost," Fraser turns his attention to a dunghill. The poem opens in mock lament: "Auch, you dreary dunghill," he writes, using deliberately clunky rhyme and exaggerated disgust. The pile is "maulish," "reeking," and "of such little renown." But the setup is a sleight of hand. What follows is a tale about "wee Davey" evading police by diving headlong into the compost's "maw." Davey burrows in, disappears, sleeps soundly, and the moment is immortalized with a backyard shrine to the compost itself. The story is amusing, and Fraser treats it with the rhythm and reverence of a tale of heroism. It's a deeply Scottish joke: elevating the low, memorializing the mess, and granting foolery its proper due.

"The Kid Has Talent" caries this nostalgic impulse into more personal territory. It opens with a child painting a schooner on the inside of an oyster shell, then follows him through piano lessons, cross-country drives, car polish, heartbreak, and banjo serenades beside English Bay. It is a life rendered in snapshots, full of detours and delights. The voice is affectionate; the details are precise. And the closing lines circle back to that first image: "[He] came home at night, to his painting / on the inside of half an oyster shell." It is a strange and tender ending, one that resists explanation but lingers. Like so much in this collection, it is not trying to instruct. It offers a memory and asks us to keep it.

On Language and Form

The language of this collection is clear, musical, and often grounded in the cadences of speech. It is unpretentious, but never careless. Rhyme arrives playfully, sometimes unexpectedly, and meter shifts to follow the contours of thought and feeling. Line breaks do not obey formal rules so much as emotional logic. Rather than aiming for polish, the writing favours directness and immediacy. Its strength lies in the voice: steady, attentive, and deeply committed to the work of remembering.

That voice is at its most distinctive when it brings together humour, narrative, and emotional presence. "The Border Tree" is a clear example. The poem transforms a property dispute into a lyrical monologue spoken by a tree caught between two neighbours. Its tone is formal, even courtly at times: "Neighbours, I sheltered you both, / I protected you from sun and rain." Yet the poem moves easily between sentiment and satire. The tree speaks with dignity about its unexpected demise and its posthumous role in legal history: "I shall live forevermore / as a legal precedent." The humour is undeniable, but it does not cancel the pathos. The tree's voice is wounded, puzzled, and strangely wise. The poem showcases Fraser's ability to shift tone mid-line, to mix narrative with character, and to play within poetic form without losing emotional resonance. The result is a story that is gently amusing and quietly moving, told in a voice that is both theatrical and deeply humane.

Other poems approach form with a lighter touch. "WHY is SNOW so WHITE?" turns a question of surface into a meditation on perception. It opens in curiosity and ends in something closer to reverie: "the whiter the white, / the greater my reflection. / While I seek but / cannot find perfection." The stanza chases no answer. It pauses in the moment of unknowing. The poem's form reflects this; it is spare, slightly off-balance, suspended. It understands that mystery is not always something to be solved. In "Old Fashion," Fraser plays with poetic inheritance. The poem blends commentary and narrative reflection, shifting between academic and conversational modes. It moves through references to beat poetry, McLuhan, Hemingway, and more, before arriving at something grounded and intimate: "cottonwood fluff floating / down through the trees." If Fraser's portrait is affectionate and lightly ironic, it is also admiring. His friend's literary style may be labelled old-fashioned, but Fraser sees in it something enduring: clarity, feeling, and craft. The poem's hybrid form, part monologue, part tribute, part *ars poetica*, echoes its subject. It suggests that what lasts and is of value is that which stays true to experience.

Finally, in "As Sun Sets Through Church Glass," Fraser offers something more ceremonial. This is one of the more formally structured poems in the collection, drawing from classical meter and literary allusion. Figures like Austen, Dante, and Coleridge appears as guiding voices. The couplets are regular and musical, and the scene—a bride stepping into a sunlight chapel—is treated with reverence and intimacy. The tradition being honoured is both poetic and personal. The poem affirms that formal language need not be impersonal. It can also be gesture of care.

Final Words

This collection sets aside literary fashion and technical display. In their place, it offers something rarer: a voice that speaks with clarity, affection, and a deep sense of presence. The poems stretch as feeling deepens. They turn to rhyme, reflection, and the occasional philosopher—not to impress but to invite. Even the smallest gestures carry the weight of intention: a pun shared in affection, a line of prayer offered in earnest, a remembered phrase preserved like a talisman.

What holds these poems together is emotional honesty, a desire to honour what has mattered and to preserve it in language. These poems are for those who are gone, and for those who remain. They speak to anyone who has tried to name what feels inexpressible, and to those who keep returning to memory not for answers, but in search of connection.

More than anything, this collection stands as a testament to the act of writing. It trusts that what we remember, we keep alive by telling. And perhaps what endures longest is the voice that continues to speak with care and conviction.

May these poems keep speaking.

Rebecca Sheppard,
PhD English Literature,
University of British Columbia

Poems

Prophecies

In the background of my selfie
lies the snow-covered sands off
Spanish Banks, beyond is the Salish Sea.
All is anticipation and alliteration.

When our Lions become winter snow-free
the coming flood from the melting Greenland glaciers
        will not be held back by you or Canute or the
        cliffs of Jericho.

"A catastrophe," sayeth David Suzuki
also read T.S. Eliot's *The Waste Land*, "Fear death by
        water" or heed God's advice to Noah, "build an
        ark for I will bring a flood of
        waters upon the
        earth."

People, what more prophecy do you need to convince
        you to correct your
        wasteful ways?

Response

We hear, see, and disagree with
the opinions of your chosen three.
Besides if we are wrong,
Elon Musk's ark to Mars
is always a contingency.

Perspectives

I am reading the Prophet today.
I pause to watch robin eat a holly berry.
CAT,
purring on my lap, watches too.
ROBIN
appears to me as an artform,
russet breast ruffled against the
COLD,
'midst thorn and greenery.
Cat sees robin as a meat
TREAT.
We are disappointed when robin flies off.

I turn back to the Prophet,
cat loses interest,
there is no meat there.

PHILOSOPHERS
and cats sup at the Prophet's table on very thin soup.
The Prophet writes, 'In much of
TALKING,
thinking is half-murdered.'
He gets no quarrel from me,
for some of his writing
has the hollow ring of Polonius
who said to his son, "neither a
LENDER
nor a borrower be."

On the agonies and joys of life
broken down into a list —
LOVE,
Pain, Religion, etc. — the sum of what the Prophet
says is: don't dwell on yourself, interact with nature.
CAT,
napping on my lap, dreaming of
robin, purrs in agreement.

Mountain Lake

The cloudy veil was lifting,
I saw Her downcast eyes
reflected in the lake's still waters
under mist-filled skies.
The far shore's dark shadow
framed this solemn place,
suggesting to me a portrait
of Madonna's grieving face.

A faint breeze murmured on
the rippling mountain lake,
"The cloudy veil is lifting.
 Stay, stay on for Her sake."

I lingered by the dark shore
thinking nothing would be found
beyond the memory of Her downcast eyes
in the sadness all around.

I waited an hour
for the rising of the cloud.
Did the cosmos
have the power
to unwind her heavenly shroud?

The heavenly veil was cast aside
By the sun's filtered threads
colouring the mountainscape,
the evergreens, and maple reds.

To a chorus of birdsong,
the bright sky revealed
snow-capped mountain peaks
which had hitherto been concealed.

Isn't this but a pleasant sight
reaffirming a commonplace
dawn giving way to day
at earth's measured pace?

Yet, the glory of that scene when
Her Son crowns the sky
made Madonna's face glow bright
bringing pleasure to my eye.

I find myself a witness
to a homecoming so surreal
that all my six senses feel
what reason tries to conceal.

Turtle Dove

SILENT TURTLE BLINKS AN EYE
HIS HEART BEATS WITH LOVE
FOR PERCHED ON TURTLE'S
HEXAGONAL SHELL
IS A COOING DOVE.

DOVE COOS, TURTLE BLINKS,
PRECIOUS MOMENTS GO BY
COOING DOVE TAKES FLIGHT
SILENT TURTLE SIGHS A SIGH.

THIS COULD HAVE BEEN A TRAGEDY
ACCOMPANIED BY STRINGS
BUT THAT SLOWLY BEATING TURTLE'S
HEART HAS SUDDENLY GROWN
            WINGS.

Viva Joan

HUSH,
I hear a puckish minstrel
singing his sweet lay,
a midsummer night's
dreaming on coronation day.
COME
sings he, set a course
across the wine-dark sea
for purple picnic party
and promise of joie de vivre,
to the coronation
of one we all hold
DEAR
so, wind fill white sails
and bring our black ship near.
Lion cups we shall raise as
EMPRESS
takes her throne
amid
shouts from
wine-dark lips
repeating viva
JOAN.

An Unrepentant Husband

I drank too much wine at dinner
and woke with an aching head.
Deciding to forego my spousal
duties, I lay in bed instead.
The children insisted on playing,
the idea appealed to me,
I left them to play with you, dear,
and joined friends on the first tee.

We visited once in the country.
What was one to do in the rain?
For my humour to be restored,
I suggested a risky Russian game.

These actions I have described
are but a select few
of the many that comprise myself,
to which Polonius says, be true.

You told me to apply reason,
for that should give me a clue
of where my selfish actions will
inevitably lead me to.

Alas, reason leads me down
another path, less trod 'tis true.
I deduce that my selfish acts,
dear, bring forth the Saint in you.

Ode to a Cement Block Compost

Auch, you dreary dunghill
Of such little renown
A box full of leavings
All mouldering and brown.
There is nothing to sing
Of glorious praise,
You maulish, reeking pile,
What a stench you raise.

Yet, it was a compost
On a night long ago
That sheltered wee Davey
When his spirits were aglow.

'Twas on a lively retreat
From the upholders of the law
Down the darkened lane he ran,
Diving into the compost's maw.

He burrowed and dug
So quietly and deep
He avoided them all
And soon was asleep.

Now that you know the story
You'll not be amazed that
The monument in Davey's backyard
Is to a compost praised.

The Word

Father Cooper, he of the cauliflower
ear, shared the word.
It echoed in St. James' vaulted dome.
It was in common usage,
and was repeated by Herb and Joan,
who as part of their wedding vows,
made the word their own.

They lived the word every day,
for it was better to practice then say.
They applied it to all they knew,
family, friends, children and
strangers too.

The word embraces life,
accepts the stumbles and falls,
reaches out to those who need a hand
and says to others we understand.

It could have been but a passive verb
had it not been kept alive
by the steady gaze of Herb
and Joan's flashing dark eyes.

Their tumultuous home
echoed with cheer,
for the old priest,
with a cauliflower ear,
reached to the heavens above
and shared with them the word,
perhaps more precious than love?

Herb at Seventy

ON SAILING OUT FROM POLIER PASS
I ESPIED THROUGH MY LOOKING GLASS
AN ILLEGAL ACT BEYOND MY GRASP —
DOCTOR HERB WAS SMOKING GRASS.

APPROACHING NEAR THE ROCKY BEACH
WHERE HERB WAS WONT TO PREACH,
I HAILED, "ARE YOU NOT IN BREACH
AND so, WITHIN THE LAW'S REACH?"

ANSWERED HERB IN HIS SEVENTIETH YEAR,
STRONG-VOICED FOR THE WORLD TO HEAR,
"I SHALL MAKE IT PERFECTLY CLEAR
WHY I SMOKE GRASS WITHOUT FEAR."

"THE LAW'S REACH SHOULD NOT EXTEND
TO GRASS OR WHAT'S A HERBIVORE?"

Ode to the Fiends *

There is much to be said about
a photo of that glorious sextet
who are clustered about a flag
coloured white and red,
featuring a maple or,
in my belief, a cannabis leaf.

Ask not who they are,
ask instead,
why they sit masked and apart so far?
Perhaps they are a secret society
whose opinions are so outrageous
they are contagious.

*a biographical book club meeting
  on Canada Day 2020, the year of
  Covid-19

Beinecke

Yale Rare Book Library, Connecticut

Here am I in Beinecke
amongst the manuscripts,
absorbing the printed word
in this gold-glazed crypt.
Granted time, I write rhyme
to record the muse's wit,
while Gail, my Conrad scholar,
mines this golden pit.

Hearts and Minds

I feel at ease when our daughter's near,
Her wit is sharp, her thinking clear.
It is always a pleasure for me
To find myself in her company.

Yet, stirred by thoughts subliminal,
Our teenager had sought body minimal.
Demons danced in her head for years
as she tried to control her fears.

To help, I tried reason, then blunder,
for if heart command,
it would break asunder.
But victory isn't won by blunder
or reason alone, it's won by
what's bred in the bone.

Our daughter, second to none,
is from a line of women who have overcome.
Mother and daughter combined
what was in their hearts
and on their minds.

Together before birth, they shared a space
where one is for both, the self is erased.
Together they released from its spell,
a spirit so fine that it conquered hell.
Together they silenced her demons, I could tell
for she has brought joy to the world. It bodes well.

Lament for a Son

On wind-lashed shores of English Bay
seagulls soar while cedars pray,
and high atop the mountain peaks
the majestic snow-capped Lions weep.

Grieving parents are overcome
by the death of their dear son.
Weeping till emotion spent,
a poet hears their lament.

"A miracle when born,
he has gone; the Lions mourn.
Could a timeless poem
bring our darling home?"

"In Donne's poem the bell tolls for you,
your son's death is your own."

"Is that all there is? There must be more."
"Dante's *Paradiso* may gain you the far shore."

"Is it possible to return to what went before?"
"Read Robert Browning's what's a Heaven for."

They then witnessed something sublime,
on Squamish winds a white cloud climbed
the North Shore mountains to comfort the Lions.

Poet's words cannot replace
nature's healing grace.

Ode to Beef Tenderloin

WHO ARE THESE PILGRIMS AT OUR OAKEN DOOR
BEARING, IN THEIR OUTSTRETCHED ARMS,
VESSELS FULL OF VIANDS AND POMMES DE TERRE,
GARLANDED WITH CAROTTES
AND HARICOTS VERT?

FROM HIGHBURY TO THE HALLS OF ALMA
PRESSING ON US THOSE AROMATIC BALMS
RECEIVING OUR PRAISE IN PSALMS
SUNG IN SWEET UNISON.

WE HAVE TASTED AMBROSIA
BARBECUED AND BASTED BY
OUR NEIGHBOURS, LLOYD AND MARGARET,
AND ARE THANKFUL.
BENEDIC NOS ET HAEC TUA DONA SUMAS PER
CHRISTUM DOMINUM NOSTRUM

Clan Fraser's Grand Tour of Scotland

From the English side of Hadrian's Wall,
Jack Fraser heard the bagpipes call.
He had heard a Scottish stag-hunting horn
fully one month before he was born.

Celtic emotion stirred quickly in him
reaching a chorus in his next of kin:
his mother Julia, his father Lauch,
and his grandparents, the older stock.

Clan Fraser on a Sheffield May morn
gathered to answer the call of the horn,
to take the highroad to Scotland dear,
to Inverness, Applecross, and Scottish cheer.

The wee bairn slept on his first night
in Edinburgh, where the moon shone bright,
full upon his sonsie face,
home amongst the Scottish race.

'Twas to the Highlands they went next,
where Scots hospitality is best.
to toast with highland dew
the home of single malt brew.

The heathered hills of Glen Affric wild,
welcomed Jack, the six-month child.
Glens, burns, and bonnie braes,
misty morns and sun-filled days.

Fort George, after Culloden, was built
to punish the people who wore the kilt,
who marched to pipes and wielded claymores,
for none were better at waging wars.

Fort George is garrisoned by Seaforths now.
The Scots are at home wielding the plow,
where dancing and piping never cease,
for none are better at keeping the peace.

Beautiful fields round Beauly town
cradle baby Jack of sweet renown
swaddled in a brown kilt, spartan,
the Clan Fraser hunting tartan.

Hi-ho to Applecross, the gathering of clans
travelling from distant Canadian lands.
A cotter's cottage, the ringing of bells
MacDonalds, Frasers, Morrisons, and Wells.

The pipes skirl a jig as the tour ends.
Martha asks, "Jack, will ye nae come back again?"
"Aye," he cries, "those are my plans
for my heart belongs in the Highlands."

And father Lauch says, "Afore we go,
raise your glasses, get a wee glow.
To Scotland, to Jack, to our clan,
to Julia, to Gail, and the grizzled old man."

Grassfire Dance

Winter snow melts in a soft spring rain,
the Cariboo will soon be green again.
Morning sun shines on a tan stubble field,
time to fire the grass to increase the yield.

I light the fire on a Sunday morn,
the wind is calm, the world at rest.
Like the calm before the storm,
like the calm before I was born.

Smoke curls from the grass,
from the flame's slow dance.
It is now as in the past,
I watch and am entranced.

Hour after hour I tend the fire,
then hunger strikes and I retire
to our nearby cabin on high
to eat and eye the puff-cloud sky.

A door shuts, a flag flutters,
an outside vent starts and stutters,
the wind is up from the west.
I pay no heed, I choose to rest.

Smoke stings my closed eyes.
Is that crackle fire grass I hear?
Caught by the wind's surprise,
soaked in sweat, I rise in fear.

Straight to the fire I go,
to the heart of the inferno,
where the wind has changed the rhyme
from three-quarters to double time.

I'm fighting the fire, inhaling the smoke,
and smothering the flames with a shovel.
I work with a will as the fire gains the hill
and my heart starts to give me trouble.

On the top of the hill stands our little house
and in it the one I hold dear.
I hope and pray she'll smell the burnt grass
arise from her couch and draw near.

I could use a partner in this lively jig
while I jump up and down on the flame.
It's perfectly true I could use a whole crew
In order this fire to tame.

Finally, my love from our cabin above,
her voice lilts through the dense haze,
"Dear, do you dance the grass fire dance,
the latest Cariboo craze?"

I'm in no man's land 'tween black and tan
where the flames separate the two.
I'm down on my knees, my breath is a wheeze
and my partner appears to be fou.
But love and luck change on the Cariboo range
as quick as a magician's wand.
The wind she dies, my love comes alive,
and lady luck deals me a new hand.

For as I lay flat on the prairie mat,
my darling soaks me in tears
and down the trail, I hear sirens wail:
it's the Lac La Hache volunteers.

Later that night, I recalled the fight
while watching the last embers die
and clearest of all that I recall
is the grass fire dancing high.

Three Score Years

Black ships sail to sandy Pylos,
King Nestor tallies his wine,
Simon Fraser counts his pelts,
surrounded by drums beating time.

I had measured time in bales of hay,
billable hours, and Friday nights
take your pick, past pluperfect.

On the high plateau of three score years
the broad Cariboo plain
ends in the Chilcotin foothills:
I am in the mountains again.
Climbing from scree to parapet,
one hand grasps the ancients,
the other reaches for the young.
Together we sing the score
the why and the wherefore.

BFF 1995, Lac La Hache.

Yorick

If God is a myth,
so be I.
Having lived in Plato's cave,
called a skull
and counting myself number one,
I had cunningly arranged my
familiars in ranks.
A wise thing to do
in a troubled kingdom.

I survived on jests,
until I lost favour.
Leaving my skull behind,
it was discovered by
Hamlet,
my talkative, disturbed Prince
and I was mythologized
by his biographer,
Shakespeare.

The Kid Has Talent

At age ten he painted
a double-masted schooner,
sailing on a navy-blue ocean,
towards a golden sunset,
silhouetted against a pale blue sky,
on the inside of half an oyster shell.

"The kid has talent."
Uncle Louis would know,
he was an interior decorator.
The kid played Mum's Bechstein too.
She was proud, but
he loved the automobile.

The fifties were the decade of the car.
The Buick weighed a ton.
He knelt behind the wheel
steering it all over White Rock,
across Canada, and back again.
It took the family five days by train,
it took him a year—
he went down all the side roads.

Dad's Chevy Malibu coupe
was better than candy.
The kid washed, polished
and road steered it.
Dad worked the pedals.

Mum bought a Ford in the fifties
to keep an eye on Dad.
Didn't do a damn bit of good.
The kid creased a fender or two
and got his licence.

Tepoorten Truck and Country Club,
automotive heaven. Set to music,
it sounded good on his banjo-uke,
chased by a beer.

We all shed a tear when Auntie died.
The kid bought a Pontiac convertible,
a schooner of a car. From its deck
he courted the sunsets on English Bay,
strumming and singing and thinking
middens of oyster shells.

He traded the convertible for
wife, house, and family. It was
a good deal, blessed by the church
photographed by Kodak.
He parked his dream until
his family grew and his next car,
Mum's green Datsun stalled
on the steep hills of West Vancouver.

Special Bets, the Volvo, lasted fifteen years.
She gave him everything he wanted;
dependability, obedience, comfort.
When she was scrapped, the kid,
now known as the Old Bastard,
said a few Hail Marys, drove his limousine
back and forth on the Sea to Sky Highway
and came home at night, to his painting
on the inside of half an oyster shell.

Hymn of Praise

Hail, King of Kilimanjaro,
Hail, conqueror of the snow,
He who was born to overcome
Every obstacle and then some.

From the jungles of Africa
From the Tanzanian plain
Rises Mount Kilimanjaro
The Goliath David would tame.

With the planning of a lawyer
And the training of a jock
With the humility of a Canadian
At 60, David climbed the rock.

The climb was long and hard,
The cold was deep and sharp,
The altitude left him gasping,
He was deprived of sleep.
Yet on August 28th, 1998
David was amongst the elite,
He stood on top of the world.
Goliath was at his feet.

Hail, King of Kilimanjaro,
Hail, conqueror of the snow,
He who was born to overcome
Every obstacle and then some.

When he returned home
To play his favourite game,
He stood over a short putt
To beat his brother again.

Pausing to wave to fans,
He blew them all a kiss,
For he knew he would still be
the King of Kilimanjaro
Even if he missed.

Hail, King of Kilimanjaro,
Hail, conqueror of the snow,
He who was born to overcome
Every obstacle but one.

The Ballad of David Hay (Fly Me to the Moon)

The liquor was flowing
and the music was playing
in his in-laws' living room.
With good friends all round him
and Nancy, his bride, smiling at him,
he sang "Fly Me to the Moon."

He loves this life he's living.
You can tell cause he keeps on giving
to his family, his friends, and his tune.
We all sang along to "Song Sung Blue,"
in the old Commodore ballroom.

He wants you to know that life's
about love and pain,
for when he belts out Downie's lyrics
and we sing the refrain,
it makes life worth living again.

There's country in his songs,
a stomped-on heart,
a sense of guts and glory,
but, when he's lonely,
he sings a sad story
full of foreboding and gloom.
Then he remembers that glorious day
When he became the groom.

Yes, the liquor was flowing
and the music was playing
in his in-laws' living room.
With his good friends all around him
and his bride smiling at him,
he sang "Fly Me to the Moon."

"Nancy, my heart is filled with your grace,
more than I ever knew.
I'll sing it again and I'll sing it again: I love you."

Flights

We
stand silent,
listening to the sound,
beating wings, flights of geese
northward bound.

My
fleeting thought
on Nature's song is
to hold your hand and say,
"To you I belong."

Your
deeper thoughts will
be revealed at home,
where nothing is concealed
when we are alone.

At home your northbound
thoughts don't include me.
Your destiny is with
the high-flying
V.

Song of Spring

From the comfort of my home,
Through glass windows facing west,
I stare unseeing on winter wind
And reflect on my nothingness.

A flick of russet red on white,
robin pecks at rowan berry,
bravely foraging frozen bough,
causing my thoughts to vary.

My eye blinks and catches there
dusted with a skiff of snow
in the garden dull and dreary
a distant figure shrouded, slow.

Here is a rare sighting, for
moving through cold flower beds
is a dancing graceful gardener
cutting off dead flower heads.

Her movements are more hurried
as the dark shroud silent falls,
stoops the gardener raking, gleaning
to the warbled robin calls.

All my lethargy has left me,
all my senses, six strong,
gather birds in coloured chorus
open-throated vibrant song.

In their midst stands the gardener,
sun reflecting golden aura,
conducting in her winter garden
wild fauna in lieu of flora.

Who is this gardener, never tiring,
stirring me from winter sleep,
keeping order where there is none,
causing me to laugh and weep?

You know of whom I sing
for many natural reasons:
Sunny, the song of spring,
a woman for all seasons.

James

Under a sapphire sky
At the end of an autumn day,
Two friends watch white sails
Crisscrossing English Bay.

The windblown boats
Churn the frothy brine,
Mimicking the cosmic cauldron
Bending the curve of time.

The North Shore mountains
Frame that spectral scene
Until peace is shattered
By a muted scream.

"I buried my son this morning.
Is there any proof, my friend,
That Jamie's return to Mother Earth
Is not his journey's end?

For I believe life is for the living,
When the spark goes, the spirit is dead.
Since I lack faith, why,
Why was I not taken instead?

James would have prayed for my soul
While for him I can only fear.
When I am gone, who will remember
That he was held so dear?"

"Your answer, my friend, is
In Donne's immortal poem.
The bell tolls for everyone,
Therefore, no one dies alone."

"That doesn't satisfy me.
I need so much more,
Proof of life everlasting before
Sailing to that far shore."

"Poets try to capture truths
That can only be felt.
Read Dante's *Paradiso*,
It may calm your doubt."

Shadows fall at water's edge,
Sails are but specks of white,
Sun leaves the mountain peaks,
Silent comes the night.

The friends are not alone
For fear intertwines
With the wonders of creation
And their rational minds.

Continue to ask questions,
As do children of five.
Continue to seek answers and Try,
Try to keep your faith alive.

In Memoriam

Writing stories about trout
rising to a fly or setting decoys
for high-flying ducks was Harold's
legacy. His credo was
      Fish and Stream.

      Kalamalka Lake, green lawns,
      Home and Garden defined
          Marybeth's dream.

          In between they raised
          four children who thrived
          on legacy and dream.
          In Vernon they remain,
          sparkling ripples on
             lake and stream.

Lawyer, forester, gardener, teacher,
Okanagan friends, sons, and daughters remember:
Harold and Marybeth's story never ends.

WHY is SNOW so WHITE?

F.H. Low-Beer poses
a cool question.
Why is snow so white?
We know why snow is white:
Wikipedia tells us it's all about
light reflection.

But why is snow so white?
There is no right answer.
The poet-philosopher
causes us to pause and think.

From the warmth
of our subjective beings,
the itch of our curiosity.
From the breadth of our
Imagination, each of us
will fashion her own meaning.

Mine is the whiter the white,
the greater my reflection.
While I seek but
cannot find perfection.

Old Fashion

Commercial Drive
is home to the old poet,
who believes that his beats,
popular in the sixties,
don't suit the free verse crowd.

Lately he's discovered
that short stories are the
McLuhan's medium that appeals
to all Canadians with
noble intentions.

His short story is about
an old man remembering
the fifteen-year-old playing
baseball, his passion.
Boy meets first love.
The poignant, touching story
ends with an image of
"cottonwood fluff floating
down through the trees."

His literary friend called
his short story Old Fashion.
I call it poetry like Hemingway's
The Old Man and the Sea.

Hear the Song of Our Son

Wednesdays were coffee at Starbucks.
I drove to Highlands at one.
Waiting for me on the porch
was Jamie, our eldest son.

He walked towards the truck,
a tall handsome young man.
He was a star athlete once
before medicine stole his élan.

He waved, flashed a smile,
he opened the truck door,
and he said, "Hi, Dad, I'm fine.
Good to see you once more."

Coffee danced in my head.
We talked, never for long,
I recited a poem and
he said he was writing a song.

> Hear the song of the crowd,
> Cradle the ball on the run
> Towards the goalpost high,
> Under the autumn sun.

He conveyed without speaking
in his own quiet way
that he enjoyed my company
and wanted me to stay.

I had other commitments,
life was moving on
with no time to wait a while
and listen to his songs.

We stopped at Highland House,
it was his group home,
he got out and said goodbye,
I told him he was not alone.

I failed to say that on Wednesdays
he taught me to walk not to run,
be patient with others,
be at peace with myself,
and to speak ill of no one.
Virtues one learns from one's father
I was learning from my son.

Fridays, home for the weekend,
he spent time in his room,
trying to silence the voices
full of foreboding and doom.
Some Saturdays he would rally
and we golfed in the afternoon.

Sundays were special for James,
from Highlands he gathered his friends.
I drove them in the purple convertible
to church where he sang his Amens.

He wanted me to attend the service.
I had attended so many before,
my prayers had gone unanswered,
I could pray no more.

Home from the service, he praised
the preacher, the sermon, and psalm.
He joined the choir, sipped some tea,
and added a verse to his song.

Song of Our Son

Hear the words of prayer,
Sing a song to His Son,
Reach for the unknown,
Peace be to everyone.

For many years he suffered,
battling the dark refrain.
There was little the doctors could do
to relieve his constant pain.

September, we repeated the cycle
we had found to be true.
Wednesdays and weekends
were days to look forward to.
Yet in the shadows stalking
was the omen of the yew.

Late September I received a call
that turned me ashen pale;
James had assaulted a policeman,
they had taken him to jail.

It was with a heavy heart that
I saw him in jail downtown.
Shaken by his lapse, he said,
"Sorry, Dad, I let you down."

I couldn't help, I could only be
a witness to his suffering.
Standing helpless by,
I let my son down with a sigh.

I said, "St. Paul's Hospital
is the safest place for you."
I was trying to protect him
from the omen of the yew.

Bruce Fraser

At St. Paul's Hospital
James would not be confined,
he left this life by escaping
through a window in his mind.

Our coffee days, the golf we played,
are but memories now
and when I walk the golf course
I remember how
we enjoyed our time together.
I value them still
for Jamie continues to teach me
his athletic skill.

Sometime in the future,
I am not ready yet,
I shall go to church where
he sought peace and pray
that his soul's at rest.
Then I shall be strong,
sit on a hard bench,
watch the world go by,
and sing Jamie's song.

> Hear the song of the crowd,
> Cradle the ball on the run
> Towards the goalposts high
> Under an autumn sun.

> Hear the words of prayer,
> Sing a song to His Son,
> Reach for the unknown,
> Peace be with everyone.

This is the song of our son.

As Sun Sets through Church Glass

AS SUN SETS THROUGH CHURCH GLASS
FALLING GOLDEN ON THE ALTAR, EACH GUEST
FACING HEAVEN'S FIERY FURNACE
SEES THE BRIDE EMERGE IN WEDDING DRESS.

TRUMPETS SOUND A TRIUMPHANT REFRAIN
AND BLESSINGS ARE SAID AGAIN AND AGAIN.

Flanked by six strong men lest he swoon,
With time to reflect upon a youth misspent
The groom stands by the Altar in the afternoon
And gazes on his beautiful bride, heaven-sent.

True as Dante's Beatrice, the bride comes
down the aisle, sweeping all doubts aside.

Slowly, the procession moves at measured pace
Towards the Altar inscribed *"omnes unum sing."*
All is serene and full of the grace
Of Angels whispering on hovered wing.

A summer's bride in a sacred room
Rapturously received by her groom,

Mrs. Bennett could not find a better catch,
For long ago each had made their choice.
Jane Austen could not write a better match,
Yet there remained solemn vows to voice.

To say before all, family and friend:
This is our beginning, this is my end.

With emotion, sweet words are said and remain.
Among the guests the men sighed and tried
To remember, are the tears for loss or for gain?
The women know and cry for joy and pride.

A late Coleridge guest prays in a dream,
"Lord, what do they say, what does it mean?"

His prayers are answered by your scribe:
"This is like Joyce's *Ulysses*, a rich Irish stew.
As for symbols too varied to describe,
Surely a metaphor will do.

"Joyce spiced his great feast with exuberant life.
Read Joyce and rejoice for husband and wife."

Backyard Tree

A fir tree grew
in our backyard.
It was our friend.
It was our bard.
And around its trunk
the children sang
a song.

Ring around the rosie.
a pocket full of posies.
A-tishoo! A-tishoo!
We all fall down.

Our fir tree fell.
In the backyard
seedlings sprang up
all around,
all around,
seedlings sprang up
all around
and the children's
children sang
a song.

Cows in the meadow
eating buttercups.
A-tishoo! A-tishoo!
We all jump up.

The Border Tree

A case comment on Anderson v. Skender B.C.L.R.

Neighbours, I sheltered you both,
protected you from sun and rain,
freshened the spring, coloured the fall,
and harboured the birds that sang.

Children played 'neath my boughs,
privacy was granted all
until a dispute between you
was settled by a chainsaw.

On that summer day, I stood
a proud silhouette
against a Victoria skyline,
a place where lovers met.

Half of me — root, trunk, and bough —
In one yard, half within the other,
but all of me was in the hearts
of those who enjoyed my cover.

Since time began, there stood a tree
upon the hallowed ground
where Eve shared with Adam
the apple that she had found.

The priest of Spring in Golden Bough
of whom Frazer wrote
dispatched the priest of winter,
but spared the Golden Oak.

Yet one of my warring neighbours
took Solomon's advice to heart,
unleashed his mighty chainsaw
and cut me apart.

I may have survived that uncaring cut
had he not been so rude
as to deprive me of half my roots
in the heat of their feud.

In this fine province of ours
where I had the good fortune to die,
my story does not end upon
the ground on which I lie.

For one of my good neighbours
having dispensed with me,
the other resorted to the courts
to determine the value of a tree.

There before the Supreme Court,
I was granted something new.
The Honourable Lloyd McKenzie
saw it from a tree's point of view.

That learned trial court judge
gave judgement from the bench
awarding $8,239 in damages
for my recompense.

On appeal, Mr. Justice Taylor
saved the damages for last,
damages were limited to trunk and bough,
my roots were not trespassed.

I was completely at a loss
at this legal surprise,
for it was the lack of roots
which had led to my demise.

Then the learned appellant judge
in recognition of my claim
shaved but $436 from the award
thus, restoring his judicial fame.

On thinking back on my fate,
I can't complain or lament,
for I shall live forevermore
as a legal precedent.

Love and Miracles

MY LOVE IS LIKE
A SCARLET ROSE
BLOOMING
IN HER SNOW GARDEN.
HOW OR WHY,
GOD ONLY KNOWS.
LOVE AND MIRACLES
ARE HER SECRET.

VICTORIA'S LEAFLET
CLAIMS TO KNOW
LOVE'S SECRET.
DON'T YOU BELIEVE IT.

Amour

In our sun-glad garden,
next, the sheltered shade,
roses and beebalms
grow in the tree-circled glade.

"The sun is hot and
the Spring is bright,"
she said from her room above,
"but where oh where is Love?"

"I am here," Love replied,
"nestled in our flower bed,
budding to bloom again,
white petals tinged with red."

Siwash Rock

On a moss-dappled rock
rising from the sea,
green boughs shimmer
on a gnarled fir tree.
Sword fern and salal
cover the ground
amid thimble and
huckleberry.

Slh<u>x</u>í7lsh Rock:
watching over
our children's
beloved country.

Saltspring

THE ORCA-STRATED PLAY OF WHALES
ON A LONG BAY SUNDAY IN THE RAIN
ROLLING, DANCING, AND BREACHING
TO THE FORLORN CRY OF THE LOON.

NATURE PLAYS ON THE SENSES
ALL APPEARS SERENE
WHY THEN DO I SMELL FEAR
AND THINK OF IMPENDING DOOM?

A HIGH-PITCHED WHINE OF ENGINES
CIRCLES THE ENDAGERED POD.
"ONLY CHILDREN AT PLAY, YOU SAY.
THEY'LL BE EXTINCT SOON."

MAN'S INTERFERENCE IN
NATURE'S BALANCED WORLD.
A QUESTION OF SURVIVAL.
WHOSE?
A PLAY ON WORDS.

Their
Mutual Friend

He was dressed like a brave,
she had a feather in her hair.
They danced to "Mack the Knife,"
then she disappeared,
he knew not where.

He found her outside
with their mutual friend,
taking in the night air.

In a fit of despair,
he took her in his arms,
carried her home,
and proposed to her there.

At their wedding, they received
congratulations with affection
from their mutual friend,
a nomad wandering on the
bleak plain of social rejection.

Decades later, after she of
the feather had gone forever,
he asked their mutual friend,
"What happened then and
there in the night air
a long time ago?"

"She told me," he said,
"I am going to marry my Brave."
She was young and fair,
he was stubborn and slow,
a long, long time ago.

A Covid Christmas Eve Treat

Archangel Carol foretold of a parcel on my doorstep. I made bold
       to go down the stairs ever so quick, to see if it was baby
       Jesus being delivered by St. Nick for in these days of Covid,
       Christmas, and mixed messaging, how was I to know what
       Santa would bring?

On my stoop was a colourful sack that must have dropped off Santa's
       back. I ran to the street and called out his/her name, but all
       my shouts were uttered in vain.

What was in this parcel so carefully swaddled,
was it something to be drunk or coddled?
Aero helped me unwrap the colourful sack
that had just dropped off Santa's back.

There it was for us to see: a doubly delicious delicacy. A quiche
       from Carol for my Covid Christmas Eve treat plus a biscuit
       for my dog, Aero, before we sleep.

Resurrection

When her preserved
remains were revealed,
a jewelled crucifix in a closed fist
told of a tragedy, long concealed.

Her last thoughts had been fixed
on that jewelled crucifix.

Had she prayed that her soul be
saved as she sank into the boggy
mire fated to be her lonely bier?

Or, with plunder in hand, did she flee
from the law into a thick Irish fog
only to sink to her death in that bog?

Sinner, saint, thief, or penitent
either, or; pay it no mind,
her untimely death was unkind.

Suggestions for My Eulogist

Perhaps you needn't report
that I have passed on
to God's spiritual resort.

I quietly suggest that you tell
my celebrants not to guess
the whereabouts of my final rest.

Remind them, my kind eulogist,
that my words exist, my spirit is free,
death is not the end of me.

A Chilcotin Saga by Bruce Fraser

❝ He saw the Creator's amphitheatre: the wild white potato flowers appeared as snow on the hills surrounding the stage, a bare grass-covered area with two small lakes glistening side by side in the afternoon sun. In Noah's mind, they were the eyes of the mountain — a connection to the spirits of their ancestors. ❞

The Hanlon family has many problems facing them, but drawing strength from the land beneath them, they take on challenges from rodeo grudges to a small-town sheriff with a chip on his shoulder, from betrayals to loss, from cancer to a presidential candidate with a secret that crosses borders.

A Chilcotin Saga explores the mysteries of the vast canvas of the rugged Chilcotin region of British Columbia through the lens of a family whose roots, lives and hopes are embedded in its soil.

On Potato Mountain

The unforgiving winter of the Chilcotin envelops young Noah Hanlon, on the run after being charged with murder. Moving across the endless terrain, he reconnects with his Indigenous heritage while hoping to find the real killer.

The Jade Frog

Secrets start to change lives until, suddenly, a mysterious death triggers deeper upheavals. Questions haunt the people of the Chilcotin, with the divinations of an artist-shaman and the studies of an English teacher offering the locals their best chance to find out the truth.

Noah's Raven

A billionaire presidential hopeful's route to the White House weaves a twisted path to the vast Chilcotin. History and the region will change forever if an Indigenous elder can't overcome personal tragedy to fight for the land he loves.

Also by Bruce Fraser

Grasshopper and Other Stories

Bruce Fraser's short stories range throughout the Cariboo, ferry over to Vancouver Island and the Sunshine Coast, and fly to the Hebrides, the tropics, and beyond. A vast cast of characters fill out the world of Fraser's stories in this collection of writings from throughout his career.

About the Author

The poet and author Bruce Fraser was born in Vancouver and raised in the border town of White Rock. Educated at the University of British Columbia, he practised law in Prince George and Vancouver. His Chilcotin trilogy: *On Potato Mountain*, *The Jade Frog*, and *Noah's Raven* was influenced by the Indigenous peoples living in the Cariboo Chilcotin, where he has a ranch.

Fraser's poetic mix causes us, at times, to weep or to laugh out loud, to question God, and to be at one with nature. His poems touch on the closeness of family and the mythologies of nations on planet Earth, while shining a light on what underlies our transitory existence.

www.ingramcontent.com/pod-product-compliance
Lightning Source LLC
Chambersburg PA
CBHW051233120626
46547CB00013B/1627